MW01609143

1

Bow Ties of Bravery
Alphabet Series

Brought to you by Lise Steeves
of
Lises' Library

Bow Ties of Bravery Alphabet Series

Dedication

The Bow Ties of Bravery series is dedicated for those of you looking for something a little different.

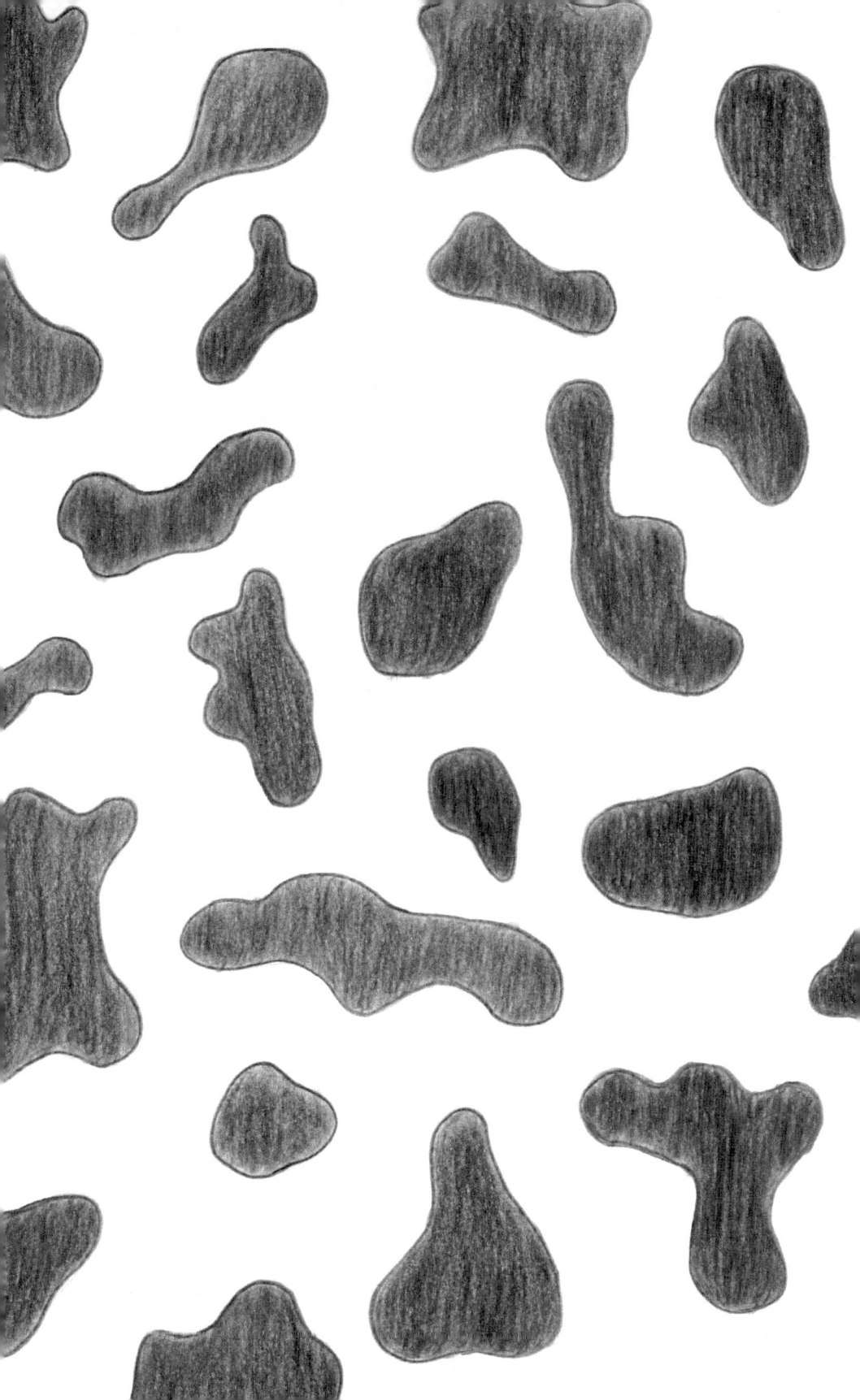

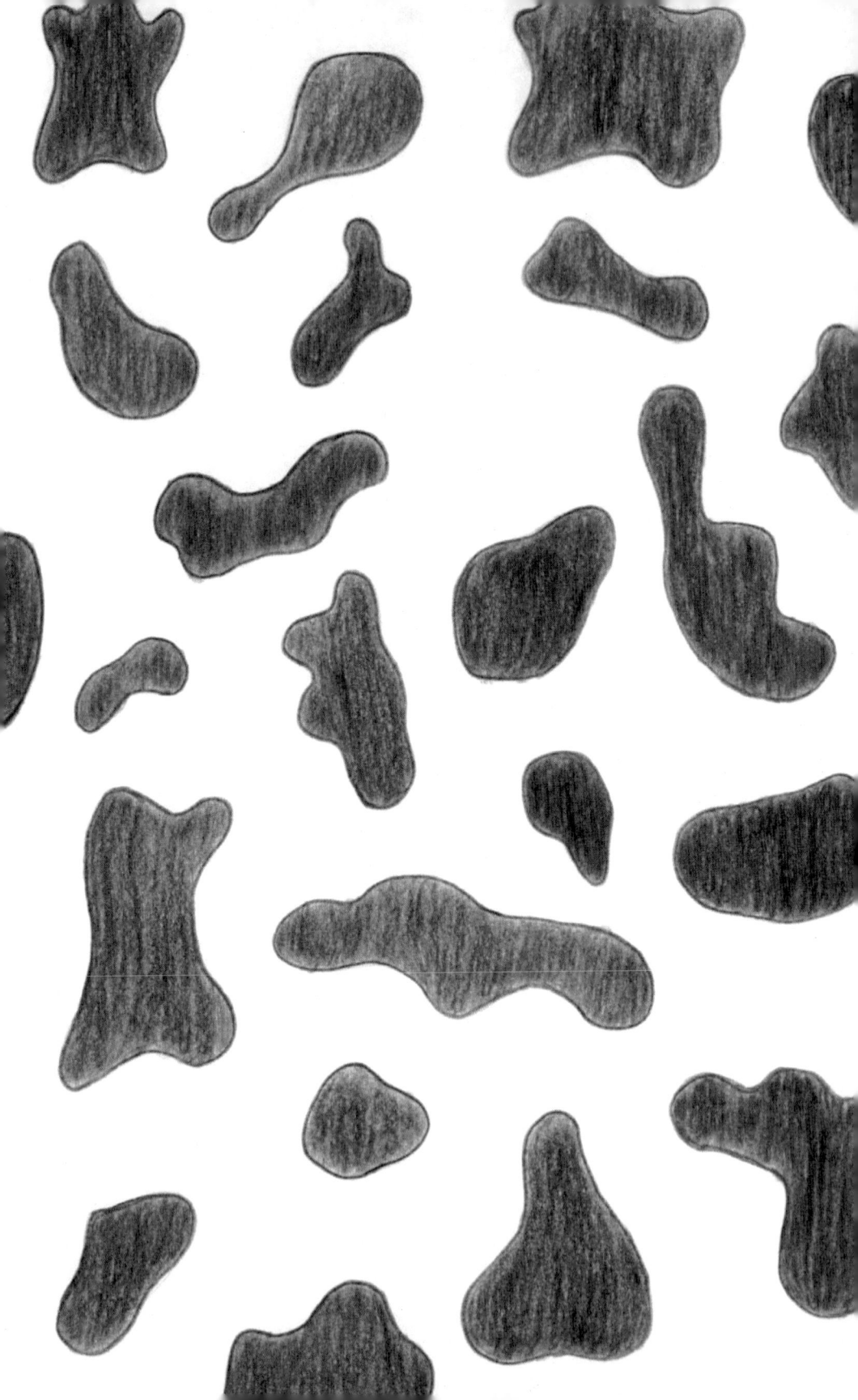

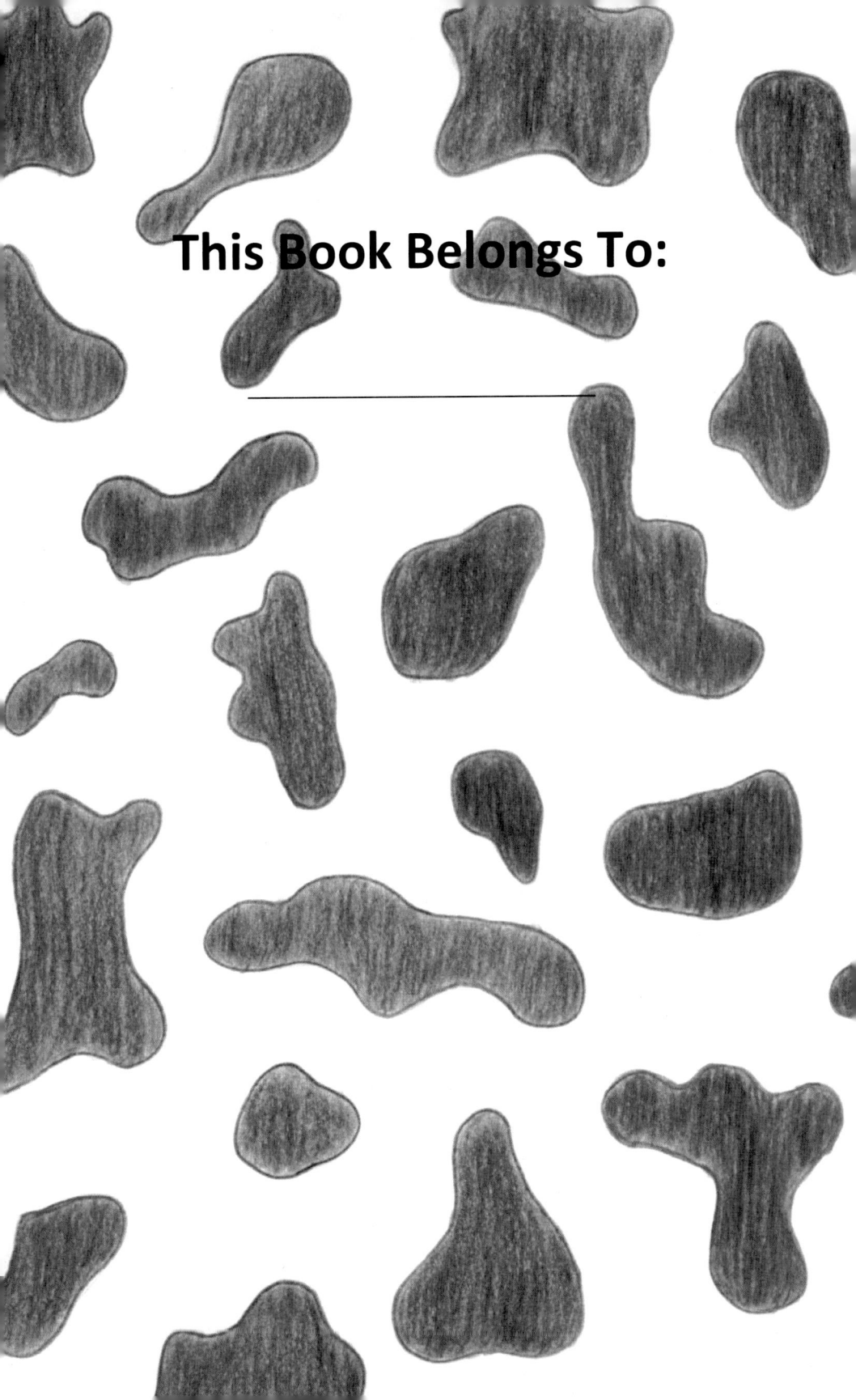

This Book Belongs To:

_____

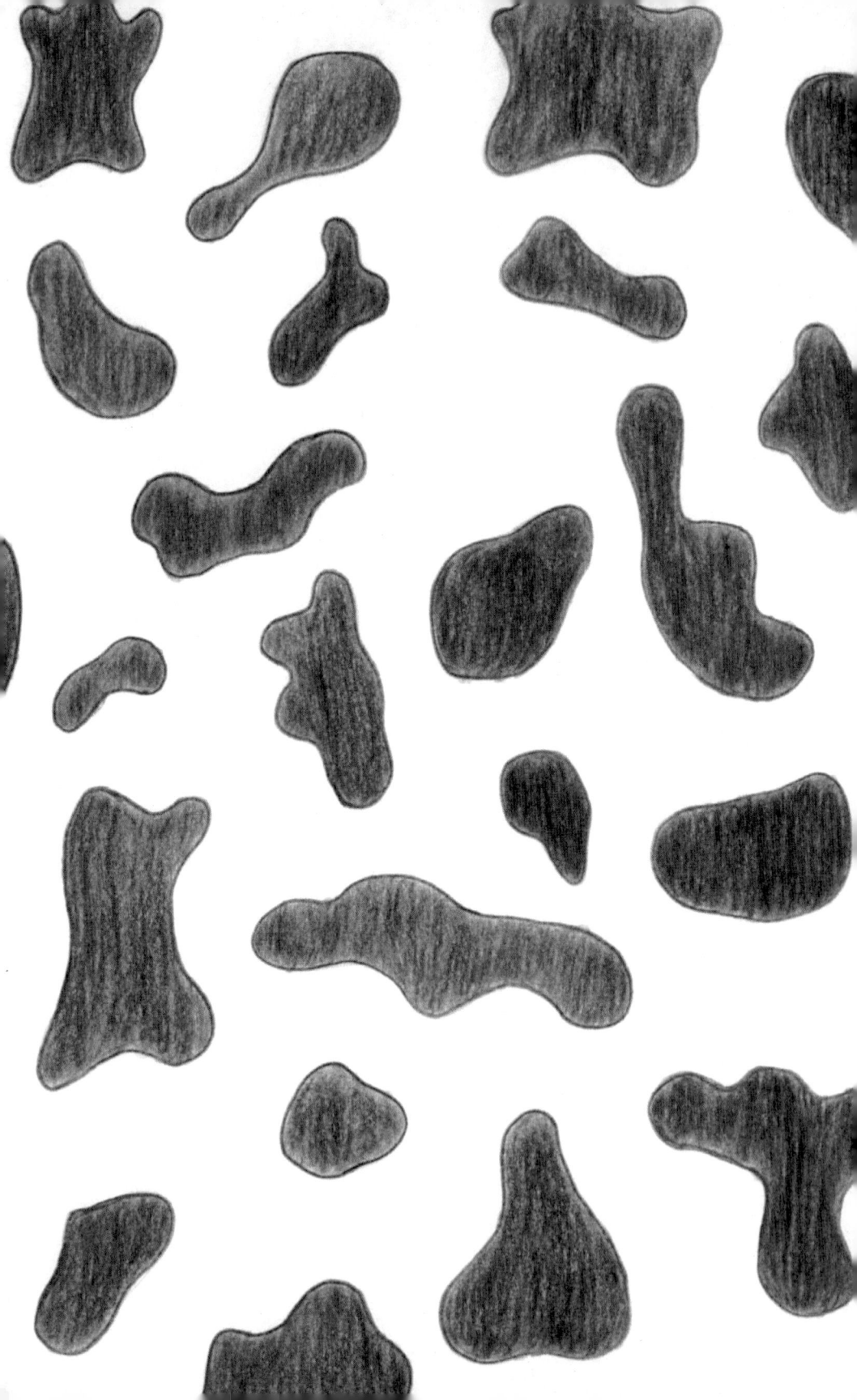

Gigi The Giraffe

Gigi Is Genuine

Written & Illustrated
By: Lise Steeves

Every Morning Gigi groomed herself before she left the house. Gigi knows it's important to present her best self to the world.

"You look great today Gigi," Momma G greeted.

"Thank you," Gigi smiled.

"Where are you off to?" asked Poppa G.

"I'll gallop to the grazing grounds," replied Gigi.

"Have a great time," said Momma G.

"Hello George, Giselle!" said Gigi

"Oh Hello Gigi," they were both surprised at Gigi's appearance.

Gigi noticed George gawking at her.

"What's the matter George?" asked Gigi.

"Are you feeling okay?" George questioned.

"I feel great, why?" said Gigi.

"Your spots are gargantuan. I think you're sick," huffed George like a know it all.

"I'm not sick," protested Gigi.

"You better see a doctor," said George.

"George, don't be so judgmental," Giselle snapped.

Gigi ran away feeling embarrassed.

"Gigi!" Giselle called after her.

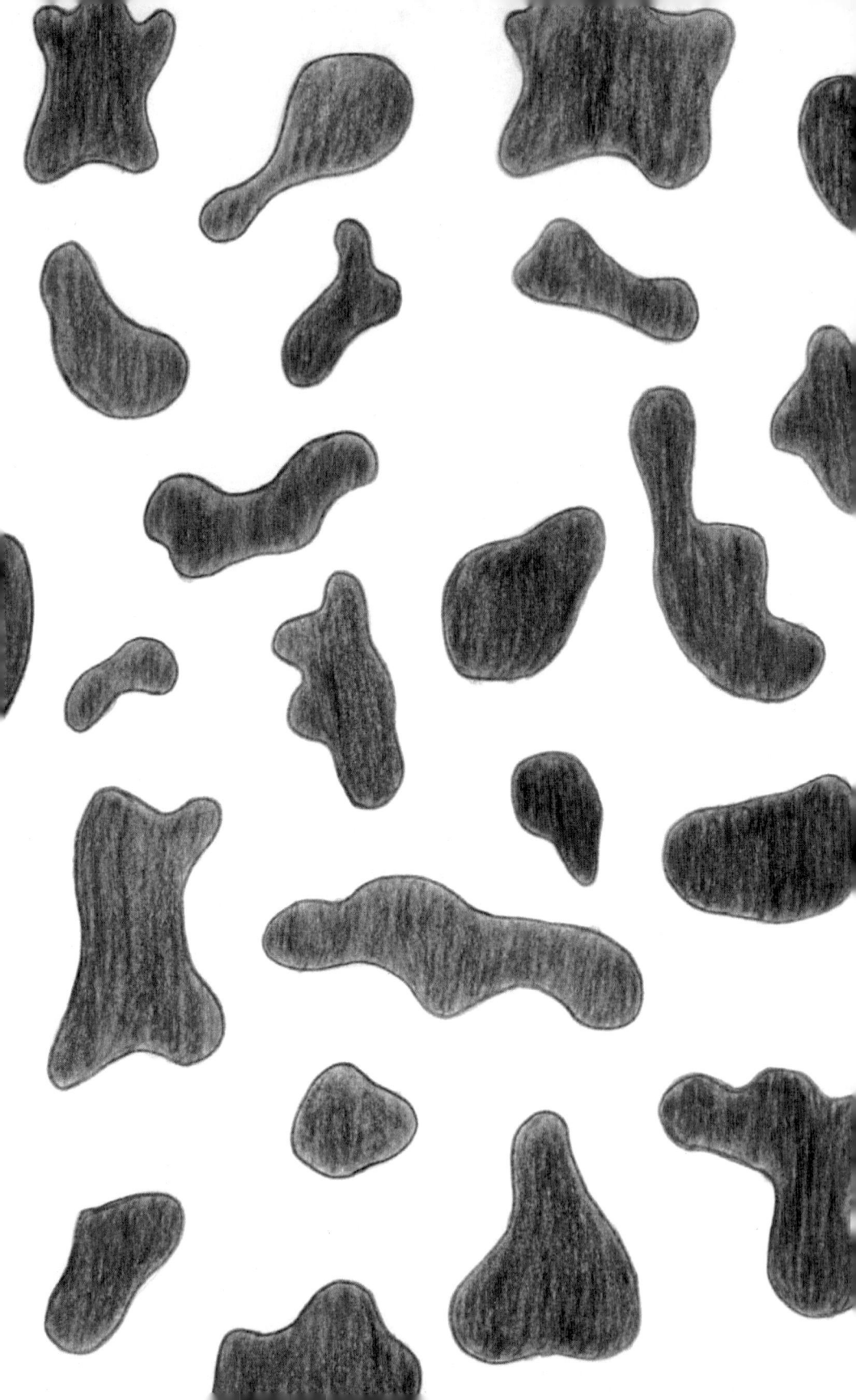

Gargantuan means

1. Very large

2. Biggest of Big

Gigi looked at her spots.
"Maybe they are gargantuan,"
she thought.
"But does that matter to me or to
others?" Gigi asked herself.

"Good day Gigi!"

Gigi glumly replied, "Good day Uncle Gary."

"What's wrong Gigi?" asked Uncle Gary.

"I don't like my spots," said Gigi.

"Hmmm...If you rub green leaves on them they will go away," snickered Uncle Gary.

"Really?" Gigi said with hope.

"Suuuure!" Uncle Gary laughed as he galloped away.

Gigi found a tree with beautiful green leaves. She wondered if Uncle Gary was right.

"If I don't try how will I ever know," thought Gigi.

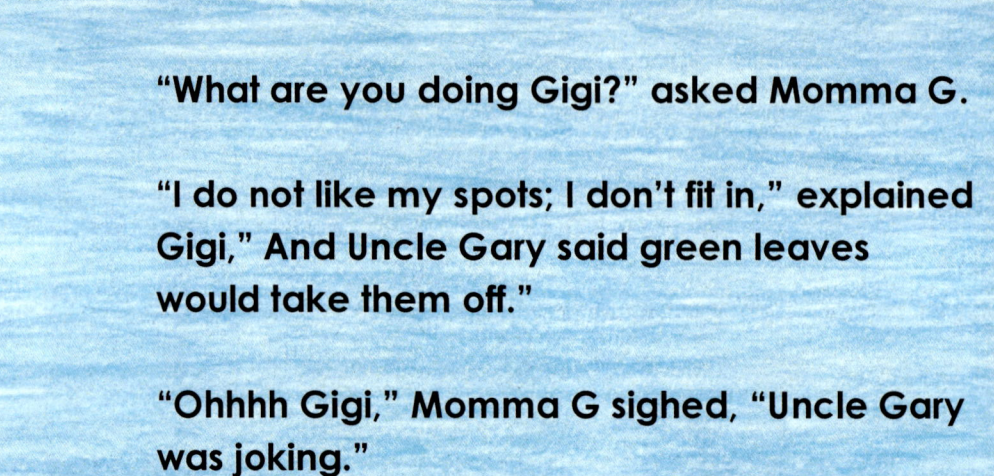

"What are you doing Gigi?" asked Momma G.

"I do not like my spots; I don't fit in," explained Gigi," And Uncle Gary said green leaves would take them off."

"Ohhhh Gigi," Momma G sighed, "Uncle Gary was joking."

"In life there will be times when you don't fit in with others."
"That just means they are not the right friends for you."
"They do not see the genuine giraffe you are." Explained Momma G

Genuine means

1. Being honest with yourself.

2. Being yourself and not someone you think others want you to be.

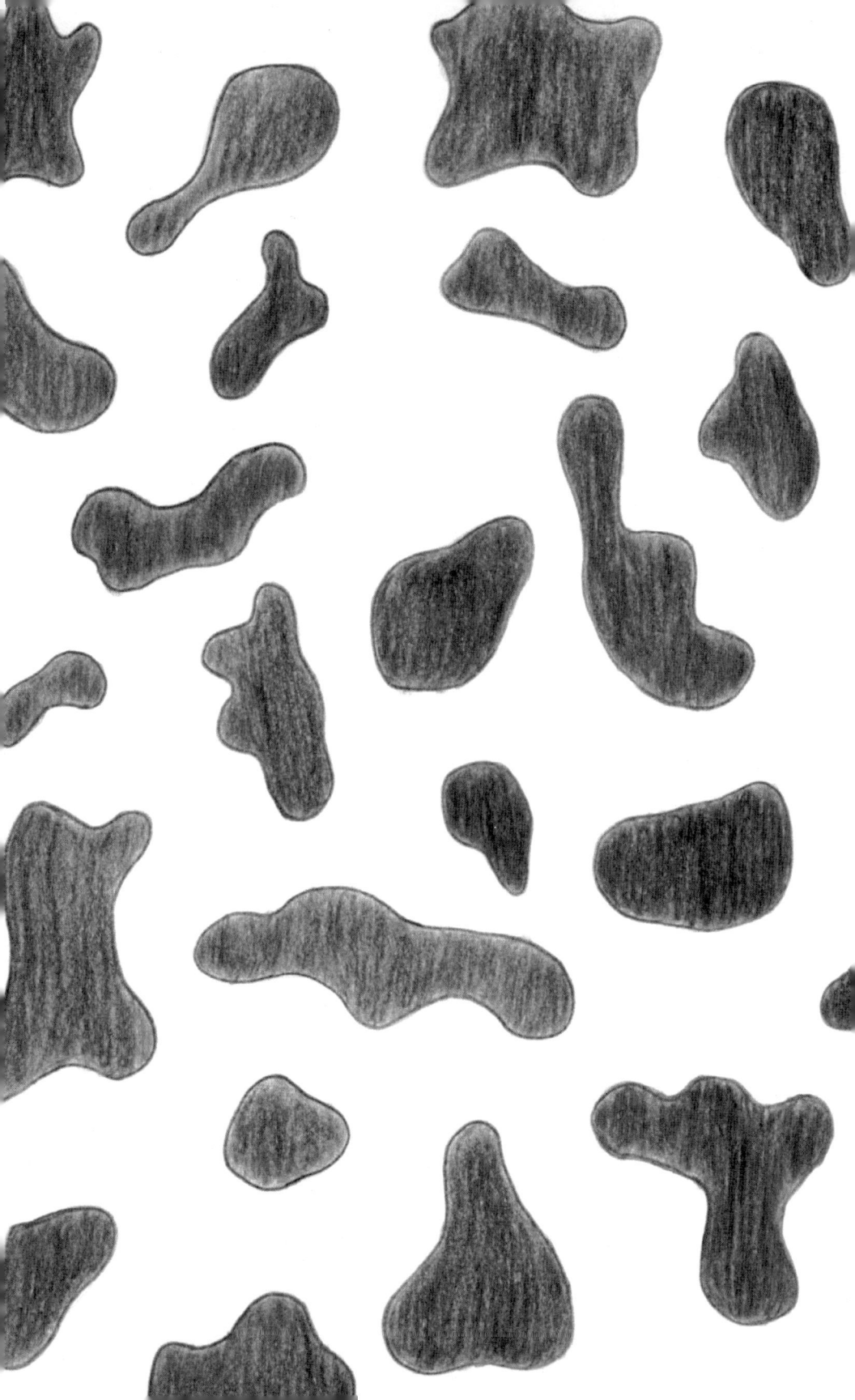

Gigi understood that she was growing up and many things would change.
As she looked in the mirror she noticed one thing that would not change; her beautiful Bow Tie.

This gave her a great sense of comfort.

Gigi decided to not let change scare her from living a genuine life.

"Hello Giselle, George," greeted Gigi.

"Oh look, it's a Gooober Globber Giraffe," George whispered.

"I heard that George.....if you don't like the way I look, then don't look at me. I don't want to be your friend if you're going to make fun of me," Gigi replied.

George snorted "Whatever," and walked away.

"Gigi, I'm so proud of you," gleamed Giselle.

"That was not easy," said Gigi. "But I do feel pretty good about standing up for myself."

"Gigi…..I like you just the way you are," smiled Giselle.

"Thanks for being a genuine friend Giselle!" said Gigi.

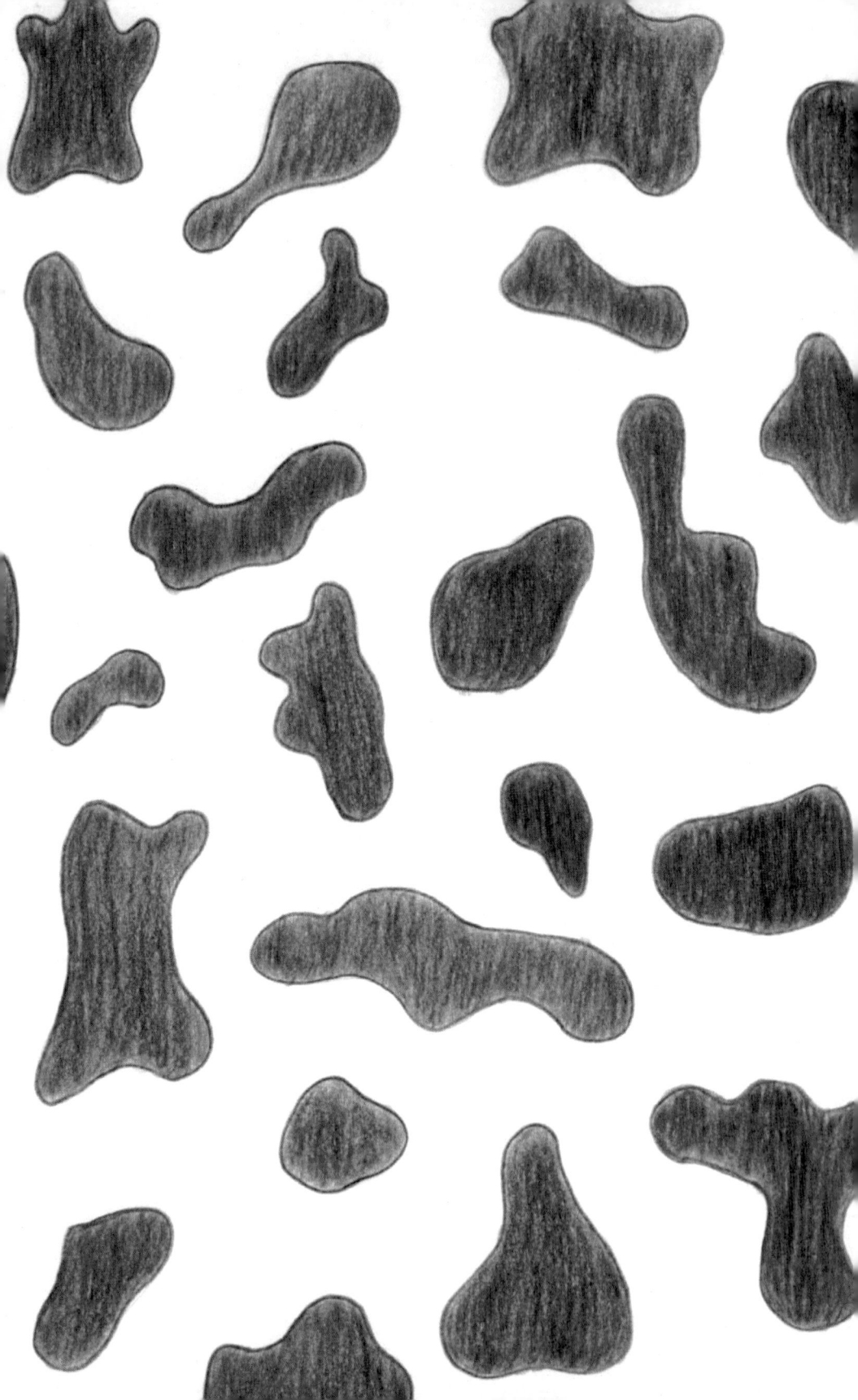

Question & Answer

1. What did George say was different about Gigi?

2. Was Uncle Gary helpful?

3. Who hurt Gigi's feelings?

4. Was talking to Mamma G helpful?

5. Did Gigi question herself?

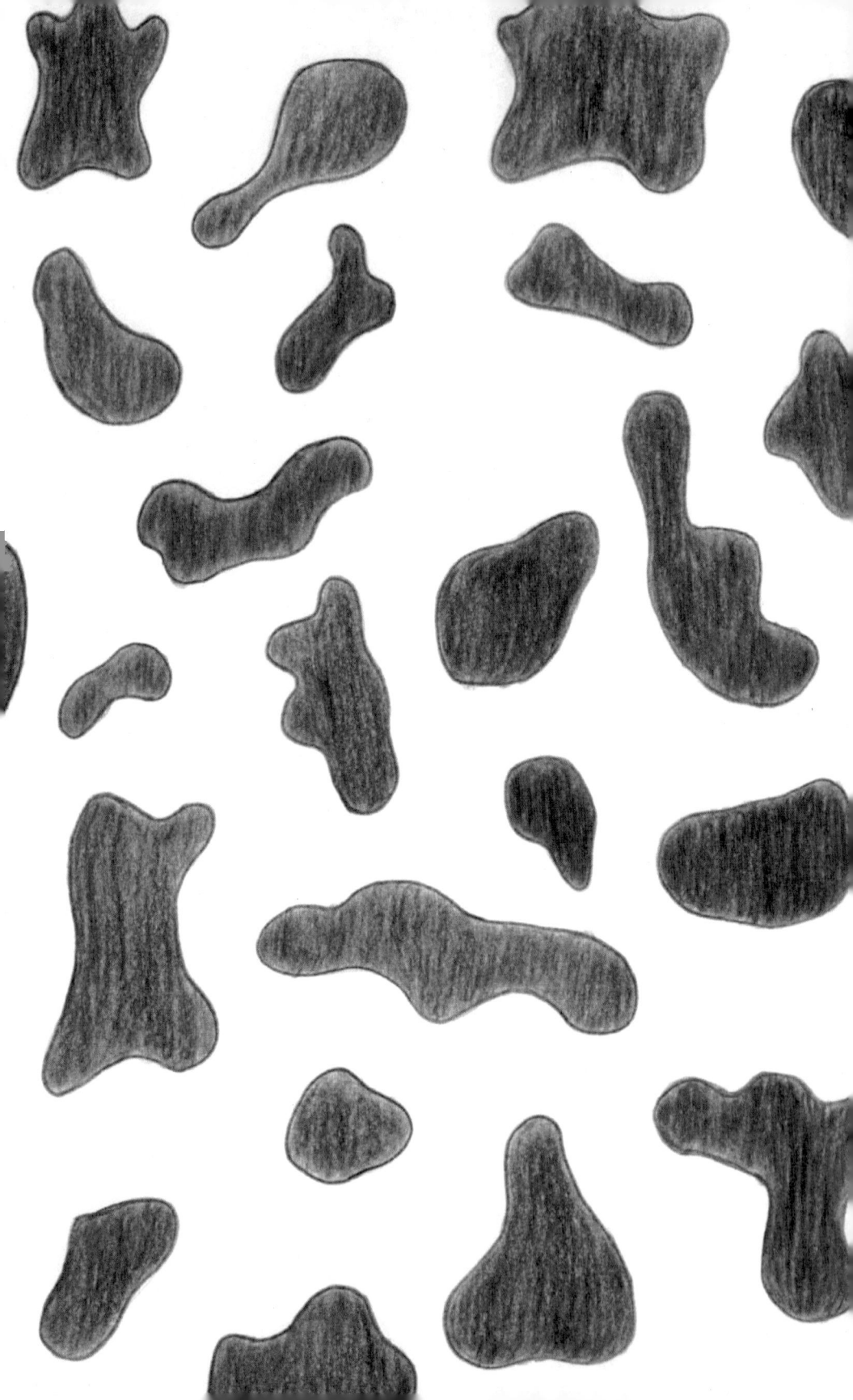

Question & Answer

6. What will stay the same for Gigi?

7. Did Gigi stand up for herself?

8. Is George a true friend?

9. Is Giselle genuine?

10. Is Gigi Thankful for having a genuine friend?

Lise Steeves is a published writer. Miss Steeves' first publication came out in the late 1980's with her letter "To the Unknown Soldier" through St. Benedict Catholic School. Writing has always been a dream of hers and she is happy to bring it to you now under "Lises' Library", the "Bow Ties of Bravery Alphabet Series."

The Bow Tie of Bravery is there for all of us in good times and bad. Whether it is visible or imaginary it is there to help give us grace, strength and courage as we face life while we grow.

First in the

Bow Ties of Bravery Alphabet Series

By Lises' Library

Next in line for the

Bow Ties of Bravery Alphabet Series

By Lises' Library

Coming soon

Bow Ties of Bravery
Alphabet Series

By Lises' Library

Made in the USA
Monee, IL
30 September 2022

14728081R00031